Shipwrecks of South Devon

Richard and Bridget Larn

Bossiney Books · Launceston

First published 2000 by Bossiney Books
Langore, Launceston, Cornwall PL15 8LD
This reprint 2005

ISBN 1-899383-35-2

Acknowledgements
Our appreciation is extended to the many early photographers of shipwrecks in Devon, as well as to the collectors and museums who have made this book possible. In particular we wish to acknowledge and thank the Salcombe Museum; the Torquay Library; Plymouth City Museum; Imperial War Museum; Elder Dempster Shipping Line; Western Morning News Co Ltd; Illustrated London News; Joshua Behenna, Slapton; Clive Carter, Penzance; R Rossiter, Paignton; G Dunn, Torquay; A Tucker, Dartmouth; B Salmon, Wembury; L Carlile Davis and Peter Mitchell, Plymouth; and the late David Murch, Salcombe.

Map by Graham King
Printed in Great Britain by R Booth Ltd, Mabe, Penryn, Cornwall

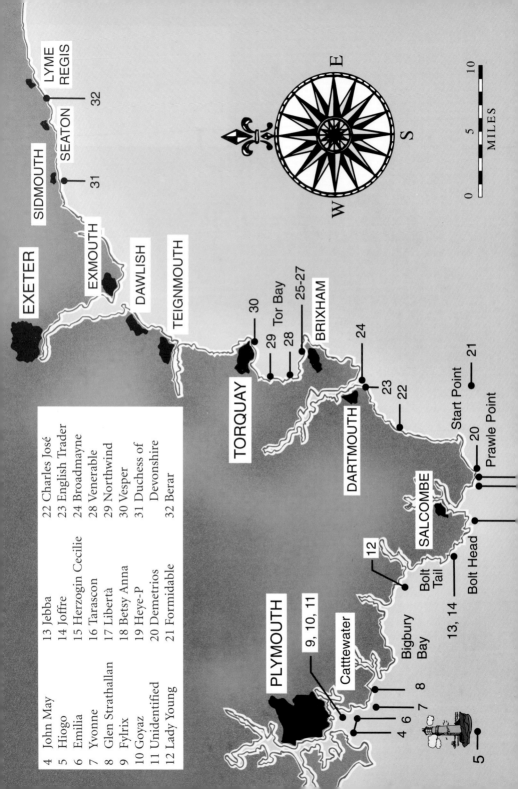

EXETER

LYME
REGIS

SIDMOUTH

SEATON

32

31

EXMOUTH

DAWLISH

TEIGNMOUTH

E

W

S

0   5   10

MILES

TORQUAY

30

29   Tor Bay

28

25-27

BRIXHAM

24

DARTMOUTH

23

22

SALCOMBE

Start Point

21

20

Prawle Point

Bolt
Tail

13, 14

Bolt Head

Bigbury
Bay

12

PLYMOUTH

9, 10, 11

Catttewater

8

7

4 6

4

5

4   John May
5   Hiogo
6   Emilia
7   Yvonne
8   Glen Strathallan
9   Fylrix
10 Goyaz
11 Unidentified
12 Lady Young

13 Jebba
14 Joffre
15 Herzogin Cecilie
16 Tarascon
17 Libertà
18 Betsy Anna
19 Heye-P
20 Demetrios
21 Formidable

22 Charles José
23 English Trader
24 Broadmayne
28 Venerable
29 Northwind
30 Vesper
31 Duchess of
     Devonshire
32 Berar

INTRODUCTION

The coastline of south Devon bears little resemblance to its counterpart in the north. Not only is it longer – 90 miles compared with 62 – but it has seven havens or ports. These are Plymouth, Salcombe, Dartmouth, Brixham, Torquay, Teignmouth and Exmouth; the north has Ilfracombe, Barnstaple and Bideford.

The geography of the two coastlines is quite different. The harsh north is dubbed with good cause 'The Sailor's Grave' or 'The Iron Coast', its few remaining trees so flogged by unremitting gales that they bend permanently away from the coast. The south is entirely different. Its cliffs are less tall and steep, and the coastline is generally less severe, the headlands intermixed with numerous sandy fishing coves and beaches.

It also has a far larger population, more rescue services and those all important 'harbours of refuge' which have saved countless vessels from shipwreck over the centuries. However, in spite of this, the south has a staggering *minimum* of 1,425 recorded losses or 15.93 shipwrecks for every mile of coast between Plymouth Sound in the west and Seaton in the east, while the north has just 8.25 wrecks per mile. This reflects the volume of shipping using the English Channel.

Every type of vessel imaginable, apart from a naval aircraft carrier or cruiser, has been lost along this treacherous stretch of coast. They range from galleons and pirate ships to coastal smacks, ketches and schooners, East Indiamen, steam colliers, tramps, tankers, liners, hospital ships, submarines, and even a battleship. And every commodity used by people – from beer to boulders, minerals to manure, wine to wool – have all been carried in these waters. Although infrequent, shipwrecks still occur: the late 1992 December gales put the 9,705-ton Panamanian *Demetrios* ashore near Prawle Point, where she broke her back in only a matter of hours.

Early photographers who created several of the photographs in this book put themselves at very real personal risk when they went out with heavy cameras and tripods to lonely and remote parts of the south coast to capture their pictures in hurricane force winds, heavy rain or fog. We owe them all a debt of gratitude for creating these historic images, many of which were taken well over 100 years ago.

Below: The only steamship wreck on the Eddystone Rocks, the ss *Hiogo* was a new vessel bound from London for the Cape of Good Hope and Japan, with six passengers and a valuable general cargo. She was due to have called at Falmouth to embark four more passengers and mail, having left London on 28 September. But at night between 2 and 3 o'clock, she drove ashore 300 metres from the lighthouse on 1 October 1867. Heading straight for the light, the Second Mate pleaded with Captain Bainton to order a change of heading, but even when within only metres of the reef the junior officer refused to countermand his orders by altering course.

The *Emilia*, a brand new steam tug only completed in February 1933 for the naval dockyard at Malta, left Glasgow for Devonport and arrived off Plymouth breakwater on 6 March. A severe gale and heavy seas obscured the warning lights on the stone structure, and she drove ashore on its seaward side. Fortunately she went beam on so that her crew could scramble over the boulders to safety. At the next suitable high tide HM salvage tug *Restorer* managed to pull her clear and, after repairs at Devonport dockyard, the *Emilia* eventually reached Valetta harbour.

Plymouth's most spectacular sailing shipwreck: the four-masted bar-quentine *Yvonne*, a steel ship of over 1000 tons built in 1900. Carrying logwood, she was on passage from Jamaica to Le Havre when bad weather and storm damage forced her to seek the shelter of Plymouth Sound at night in heavy rain on 3 October 1920.

She lost her rudder when she struck the breakwater at the eastern end near the refuge beacon, heavy seas smashing her starboard lifeboat to pieces. Using a large section of the broken boat as a raft, all the crew (except for the 60-year-old cook who drowned) managed to reach the safety of the breakwater and the Plymouth lifeboat waiting in its shelter.

Built as a fishing trawler, the ss *Glen Strathallan* was bought by the millionaire Colby Cubbin for £30,000 and converted into a luxury steam yacht – although her owner used her for pleasure less than a dozen times. She was requisitioned by the Royal Navy in World War II as an anti-submarine patrol vessel and was armed with guns and depth-charges. Returned to her owner in 1946, she became a training ship for merchant navy cadets, but when her upkeep became prohibitive, in accordance with her late owner's will, she was scheduled to be scuttled in the Hurd Deep off the Channel Islands. However, her steam engine was removed and put on display in the Science Museum, London. Then Lieutenant Commander Alan Bax of Fort Bovisand requested she be sunk near his Plymouth diving school, and on 27 April 1970 her seacocks were opened and she went to the bottom near the Shagstone.

After her cargo of granite chippings (loaded at the Dean Quarry inside the Manacles, Cornwall) shifted in heavy weather, the mv *Fylrix* of Hull took on a dangerous list to starboard in poor conditions off the Eddystone. On her way to London, she entered Plymouth Sound on 21 November 1984, anchored in Jennycliffe Bay, but capsized and sank the following day without loss of life. Contracts were invited to remove the wreck, but requests by Fort Bovisand Underwater Centre and by sport divers to leave her as a dive site attraction where she lay (she would not be a navigational hazard) resulted in the wreck remaining where she sank.

Left: Whilst the artist of this print of November 1880 did not include the name of the wreck it portrayed at Balitham, near Plymouth, it is believed to be the brig *John May* of Shoreham. She was carrying a cargo of phosphate rock from Carolina to Frederickstad when she broke from her anchor cable in Plymouth Sound on 28 October and drove onto the rocks. The man falling out of the breeches-buoy was the only fatality out of her crew of eight.

Presumably having recently been built in Britain and awaiting good weather to attempt the long passage across the Atlantic, the Amazon river steamer *Goyaz* was blown ashore under Jennycliffe, in Plymouth Sound, during the infamous 'Christmas Hurricane' of 1912.

She was later successfully refloated and saved, but whether or not she eventually reached Brazil is not recorded.

The painted gunports, some with chain-plates running across them, suggest that this unidentified wreck in Plymouth Sound, believed to have taken place in a gale in about 1860, was not a warship but an old flush-deck merchant vessel with a windlass behind her foremast. She was painted to convince privateers and pirates from a distance that she was heavily armed.

It would appear that one of her anchors lies off her port side in the shallows, and that the three visitors close to the mainmast arrived by means of the small boat alongside.

After becoming embayed in Bigbury by a south-westerly gale, the wooden barque *Lady Young* of Liverpool went ashore on 27 October 1880 on the rocks off Westdown Point, close to Bantham, from where her crew were rescued by the breeches-buoy apparatus. Shown in this photograph as she appeared two days after stranding, with men on board removing her stores and her starboard side already bilged, she went to pieces shortly after in another gale.

The subject of a quite amazing night rescue, all seventy-six crew and seventy-nine passengers of the Elder Dempster liner ss *Jebba* were rescued by ropes slung across the gap between the ship and the high cliffs near Bolt Tail. She went ashore in fog during the early hours of 18 March 1907 whilst on passage from South Africa via Las Palmas to Plymouth. The Hope Cove lifeboat *Alexandra* was launched, but heavy seas prevented her from reaching the shelter of the liner's port side. Two local fishermen, Isaac Jarvis and John Argeat from Hope Cove, climbed down the 60 metre high cliffs and rigged two bosun's chairs, by which means everyone was saved. King Edward VII later awarded both men the Albert medal. All the mail she carried was saved, as was most of her rubber and ivory cargo. She had been built in 1896 at Middlesbrough as the *Albertville*.

Another victim of fog, the South Shields tug *Joffre* went aground under West Cliff, some one and a half miles south-east of Bolt Tail, on 27 May 1925. Built in 1916 at Ardrossan, Scotland, she was 260 tons gross and fitted with a 149 hp three-cylinder steam engine. After stranding in heavy weather, her mate swam ashore with a rope by which means the local cliff rescue team rigged a breeches-buoy, allowing all ten crew to reach safety. However, her captain died shortly after from the effects of exposure and exhaustion.

Although at the time the *Joffre* looked certain to become a total wreck, she was refloated two months later, refitted and then went back into service for a further forty-one years, being scrapped in 1966.

The 3111 tons gross *Herzogin Cecilie* of Mariehamn, Finland, was a full-rigged, steel hulled, four-masted sailing ship which cost £43,000 to build at Bremerhaven in 1902. She was a crack cadet training ship for the Norddeutscher Lloyd Company for twelve years until interned in Chile at the outbreak of World War I where she remained until 1920. In 1921 she was purchased by Captain Gustaf Eriksson, who used her to make record runs in the annual 'grain-races' between Australia and Europe. In January 1936, one of sixteen ships in the 'race', she reached Falmouth in a record-breaking 86 days.

On leaving for Ipswich, she struck the Ham Stone at 4 a.m. in fog. The Salcombe lifeboat, *Alfred & Clara Heath*, took off most of the crew. She lay stranded for seven weeks before being towed into Starehole Bay, being refused permission to enter Salcombe in case she sank and blocked the harbour. Of the 52,514 bags of wheat she carried, only 464 tons were saved, the rest rotting on board and creating dreadful pollution as the wreck broke up.

Above: The 4073 tons gross *Libertà*, an Italian steamship registered at Genoa, went ashore in fog on the Mewstone, near Salcombe, on 15 February 1926. Both the Torbay and Hope Cove lifeboats were launched, but in the dark they were unable to approach the wreck, so they lay off until dawn. Rough seas meant rocket line apparatus had to be used, three men being taken into the Hope Cove lifeboat and the remaining thirty crew being saved by the local cliff rescue team. Shortly after, the vessel broke in two – as shown in this photograph.

Left: A Boulogne registered steam fishing trawler, the *Tarascon*, went aground at 5 a.m. on 23 March 1938 in Steeple Cove, two kilometres from Bolt Head. Five of her crew rowed one of the ship's boats to Soar Mill Cove where they were found by a coastguard officer, who raised the alarm. The Salcombe twelve metre lifeboat *Alfred & Clara Heath* found the remaining fifteen crew huddled together, wet and cold beneath a cliff, but could only rescue them by firing a rocket line ashore. By this means they were dragged through the sea to safety. At high tide, using blocks and tackle and the assistance of a local motor-boat, the *Tarascon* was refloated and later towed by tug to Plymouth for repairs.

Loaded with china clay shipped at Par, near St Austell, for Velsen, this is the British motor vessel *Heye-P*, registered at Ramsey, Isle of Man. She was driven ashore on Prawle Point in a gale and heavy seas on 17 December 1979 where she broke her back and later went to pieces.

Although the Dutch ss *Betsy Anna* managed to survive this stranding, after being driven between the Island and mainland of Prawle Point on 17 August 1926 in fog she leaked so badly that she sank off Portland Bill after being refloated. She was on passage from Fleetwood to Rotterdam in ballast when she went ashore at 9.15 a.m., but was pulled off by the tug *Trustee* and beached in Mill Bay at the entrance to Salcombe for repairs to her hull. Nine days later, under tow of the same tug bound for Cowes, the towing hawser parted and the *Betsy Anna* foundered. Built in 1892 at Newcastle under the name *Ashington*, her name was subsequently changed when she was sold to Dutch owners in 1905.

On passage to a Mediterranean ship-breaking yard, the mv *Demetrios* (from Long Lin in south-east Asia) parted from her tug when the towing cable snapped in huge seas, and she slowly drifted north for four miles in hurricane wind conditions force 10–12. The weather prevented the tow being reconnected, and she eventually went ashore on rocks near Prawle Point at 10.50 a.m. on 18 December 1992, breaking her back less than an hour later.

HM battleship *Formidable*, 15,000 tons, armed with four 12-inch, twelve 6-inch and eighteen 12-pounder guns, was taking part in firing exercises and being escorted by the cruisers HMS *Topaz* and *Diamond* off south Devon when she was torpedoed by the German submarine U-24 on New Year's Day 1915. She lost all steam power, which made launching her heavy boats without winches and in the dark difficult. Forty-three men got away in a barge, sixty in a pinnace and a further seventy-one in the Brixham smack *Provident*. The *Formidable* was then torpedoed again, causing her to capsize with the loss of 547 men, including Captain Loxley RN.

One of several steamships to go ashore on Slapton Sands, the Belgian collier *Charles José* of Antwerp stranded on the beach on 17 December 1933. Labourers were employed to shovel her entire cargo of coal as well as the coal from her bunkers into baskets, which were then emptied over her port side using a derrick crane and enabled her to be refloated on the following spring tide.

Whilst attempting to enter Dartmouth harbour during the early hours of 23 January 1937, the ss *English Trader* got on the Checkstone Ledge, under Dartmouth Castle, after suffering a steering gear failure. She was laden with grain from Rosario and Buenos Aires. Three tugs and HM destroyer *Witch* failed to refloat her, and she was saved only after having her bow section cut off. A new watertight bulkhead was fitted locally, after which she was towed first to Southampton and then to Newcastle where a new bow was attached. She survived until October 1941 when she was wrecked on the Hammond Knoll, off the east coast.

Outward bound for Newport News, Virginia, USA, from London and carrying a cargo of vegetable oil and wine, the Swansea registered tanker ss *Broadmayne* (3120-tons gross, built in 1888 as the *Oka*) went ashore during a full south-west gale, accompanied by heavy rain and thick fog, on the Kingswear side of Dartmouth harbour on 2 January 1921. Conditions were so bad it was impossible to launch the Torbay/Brixham lifeboat *Betsy Newbon* until 2 a.m. the next day. Meanwhile the lifeboat coxswain and his signalman walked the cliffs, located the wreck and clambered down – in pitch darkness and awful conditions – to tell the crew to stay on the ship. Sixteen men ignored the advice and followed them back up the cliff. After conditions improved, it still took the lifeboat six hours to locate the wreck in the fog and they rescued the twenty-eight crew still aboard. The ship later broke in two and became a total loss.

Above: At daybreak on the morning of 10 January 1866, following the ferocious south-east hurricane that had blown all night and was to continue throughout that day, the beach between Brixham and Broadsands in Torbay was littered with shipwrecks and debris. The photograph shows ships smashed to pieces against the wall of Brixham quay. Seven vessels were completely devastated here alone, and the floating wreckage from many more is also visible.

Overleaf: This print from the *Illustrated London News* of the time gives some idea of the extent of the damage to shipping, and the cost in lives, ships and cargo.

Above: Part of a fleet of Royal Navy men o'war blockading Brest, the *Venerable* and other vessels sought Torbay for shelter in November 1804. The admiral ordered an immediate departure shortly before dusk on the 24th, which was inappropriate since no advance notice had been given and the crews of all the warships were at their evening meal.

On board the *Venerable*, a third rate 74-gun ship, a seaman fell from the cathead into the sea; then the boat lowered to save him capsized, drowning a midshipman and two sailors. Having raised her anchor before setting sail, the ship drifted down on Paignton Ledges, at Roundham Head, where she rolled over on her beam ends and became a total loss.

The Torbay customs cutter was used to rescue survivors. All but eight men were rescued from a crew of 555. Most of her guns were recovered by the diving brothers Deane, and were later shipped to the Isles of Scilly garrison.

After stranding on a beach between Torquay and Paignton on 22 December 1964, heavy seas battered the Danish motor-vessel *Northwind*. When the gale finally abated she was pulled clear and refloated, but she had suffered severe bottom hull damage.

Below: Insured against loss for £280, the underwriters of the 24-ton Brixham fishing smack *Vesper* had to meet the full costs when on 12 December 1902 she ran onto rocks half a mile north of Black Head, near Anstey's Cove, Torquay.

Fog caused her to venture too close inshore and, after stranding, her crew rowed the short distance to the beach in their own boat.

She had been built at Brixham in 1892 by Robert Jackman in the Victoria Shipbuilding yard, behind Brixham breakwater.

The *Duchess of Devonshire*, an excursion paddle-steamer operating between Seaton and Torquay, arrived at Sidmouth on 27 August 1933 about noon carrying forty passengers, some of whom wished to disembark.

Her bow was run ashore and a small gangplank rigged to the beach, but before any of the passengers could depart a huge wave lifted the vessel, swung her beam-on to the coast and dropped her on top of some concrete steps. This tore her hull open. Her crew plugged the hole as best they could, but her pumps failed to stop the inrush of water and she was eventually abandoned as a total loss.

A victim of fog, the Italian wooden barque *Berar* of Genoa, built by W Pile at Sunderland in 1863, was carrying a full cargo of cut soft wood from Borga to Seville when she broke in two in the Channel in a force 9 gale. Her bow section eventually drifted ashore in Charton Bay, near the Dorset border, on 6 October 1896. She drove on a rock almost midway between Culverhole Point and the centre of Charton Bay, from where Captain Bertolotto and his crew of sixteen got ashore in their own boats. Her figurehead is still owned by a Sidmouth family. Local beaches were littered with timber for miles in both directions.